20 FUN FACTS ABOUT GEOLOGY

By Sarah Machajewski

Gareth Stevens
PUBLISHING

Please visit our website, www.garethstevens.com. For a free color catalog of all our high-quality books, call toll free 1-800-542-2595 or fax 1-877-542-2596.

Library of Congress Cataloging-in-Publication Data
Names: Machajewski, Sarah, author.
Title: 20 fun facts about geology / Sarah Machajewski.
Description: New York : Gareth Stevens Publishing, [2018] | Series: Fun fact file: earth science | Includes index.
Identifiers: LCCN 2017029377| ISBN 9781538211878 (library bound) | ISBN 9781538211854 (pbk.) | ISBN 9781538211861 (6 pack)
Subjects: LCSH: Geology–Juvenile literature. |
  Geology–Miscellanea–Juvenile literature. | Earth
  sciences–Miscellanea–Juvenile literature. | Children's questions and
  answers. | Earth (Planet)–Miscellanea–Juvenile literature.
Classification: LCC QE29 .M1455 2018 | DDC 551.02–dc23
LC record available at https://lccn.loc.gov/2017029377

First Edition

Published in 2018 by
Gareth Stevens Publishing
111 East 14th Street, Suite 349
New York, NY 10003

Designer: Sam DeMartin
Editor: Joan Stoltman

Photo credits: Cover, p. 1 mdd/Shutterstock.com; p. 5 Doug Meek/Shutterstock.com; p. 6 Naeblys/Shutterstock.com; p. 7 Mopic/Shutterstock.com; p. 8 Peter Hermes Furian/Shutterstock.com; p. 9 andrewpotter4/Shutterstock.com; p. 10 (igneous) Crepesoles/Shutterstock.com; p. 10 (metamorphic) www.sandatlas.com/Shutterstock.com; p. 10 (sedimentary) vvoe/Shutterstock.com; p. 11 bubblea/Shutterstock.com; p. 12 Sinasim/Shutterstock.com; p. 13 Nikitin Victor/Shutterstock.com; p. 14 Yaorusheng/Moment/Getty Images; p. 15 Joel Arem/Science Source/Getty Images; p. 16 (polished diamond) LifetimeStock/Shutterstock.com; p. 16 (raw diamond) Bjoern Wylezich/Shutterstock.com; p. 17 W. Scott McGill/Shutterstock.com; p. 18 Narongsak Nagadhana/Shutterstock.com; p. 19 Grigory Ignatev/Shutterstock.com; p. 20 CHEN WS/Shutterstock.com; p. 21 (inset) Smith Collection/Gado/Archive Photos/Getty Images; p. 21 (main) MNStudio/Shutterstock.com; p. 22 David H. Brown/Shutterstock.com; p. 23 Benny Marty/Shutterstock.com; p. 24 Paula Karu/Shutterstock.com; p. 25 (preserved fossil) NitroCephal/Shutterstock.com; p. 25 (mold fossil) InnaFelker/Shutterstock.com; p. 25 (trace fossil) kamnuan/Shutterstock.com; p. 25 (petrified wood) kdangelo/Shutterstock.com; p. 26 Machairo/Shutterstock.com; p. 27 (fossil) koi88/Shutterstock.com; p. 27 (live) Chatchai.wa/Shutterstock.com; p. 29 worldswildlifewonders/Shutterstock.com.

Printed in the United States of America

CPSIA compliance information: Batch #CW18GS: For further information contact Gareth Stevens, New York, New York at 1-800-542-2595.

Contents

Words in the glossary appear in **bold** type the first time they are used in the text.

All Those Years Ago

Earth is about 4.6 **billion** years old! A lot has happened in our world's long history. **Volcanoes** poured **lava** and steam. The steam helped create Earth's oceans. Mountains, valleys, caves, and deserts formed from the lava.

Geology is the study of Earth. This science can tell us clues about what happened at the beginning of Earth's history. It can also help us figure out what Earth's future might be! Geology helps us understand this beautiful world we call home.

These rock shapes took millions of years to form. Earth looks much different today than it did long ago!

Whole Lotta Layers

inner core ·····································●

outer core ·····································●

lower mantle ···························●

upper mantle ·····················●

crust ·····························●

The only layer people usually see is Earth's crust. It's the surface we live on!

FACT 1

From the surface to its center, Earth is made of five layers.

The outer layer—Earth's surface—is called the crust. Each

layer is made of different kinds of matter and spreads out

over the top of another.

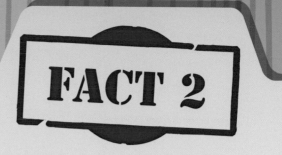
The center of Earth is a huge, hot ball of metal.

Made mostly of iron, the inside of Earth's core, or center,

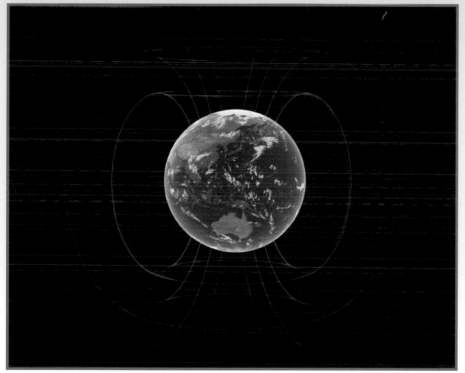

can reach burning hot **temperatures** of up to 10,800°F (6,000°C)! It stays solid because of **pressure** from its surrounding layers.

Did you know Earth's core acts like a giant magnet?

FACT 3

Scientists think Earth's crust and the rocky upper part of the upper mantle are made up of giant pieces that fit together like a puzzle.

Called plate tectonics, this **theory** says that the giant pieces of Earth called plates float slowly on top of the lower

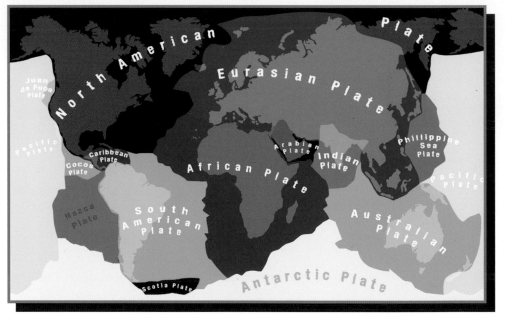

mantle. It also says that long ago, the **continents** all formed a single giant continent!

Earth's crust and upper mantle float on top of a layer of soft, hot rock.

A fault is a place where two plates meet. The crack in this picture is called a fault line. That's where pressure from down below has traveled to the surface. Often, it's where **earthquakes** occur.

Volcanoes and mountains are signs of movement and changes inside Earth.

As plates slide over, under, or into each other, pressure is created. The pressure travels up to the surface and changes it.

Rock It Out!

igneous

metamorphic

sedimentary

The three types of rocks on Earth all have different properties that scientists use to tell them apart.

FACT 5

Lava makes rocks!

Igneous rock forms when volcanic lava cools and hardens. There are two others kinds of rocks as well. Sedimentary rocks form when tiny bits of matter pile up in layers and harden over time. Metamorphic rocks are shaped by heat and pressure inside Earth.

The rock cycle is a series of processes that happen over and over again to Earth's rocks because of heat, pressure, wind, and weather. Rocks are always in some part of this cycle.

The Rock Cycle

igneous rocks

sedimentary rocks

metamorphic rocks

The floor of the ocean is made of volcanic rock!

Breaks in the seafloor release, or let out, a type of dark lava called basalt lava. Basalt is the most common igneous rock on Earth. It's also found on the moon, Mars, and Venus!

People have used basalt since ancient times to make tools and build roads.

Metamorphic rocks have wavy layers and many different colors. These properties are a sign of activity deep down below.

FACT 7

Rocks can bend—when they get hot enough!

When plates crash into each other, heat and pressure travel through the rocks and change them. The rocks soften, bend, change colors, and even change shape! These types of rocks are called metamorphic rocks.

13

Hard Rock

quartz

One of the crust's most common minerals, quartz, runs throughout these huge rocks.

FACT 8

Over 4,000 different minerals can be found on Earth!

Minerals are natural, nonliving solid matter that can be found throughout Earth's crust. They can be colorful, shiny, hard, or soft. Some even glow in the dark!

Some minerals are so soft you can mark them with your fingernail!

Other minerals are so hard that nothing can mark, or

scratch, them at all! The scale used to measure the hardness of a mineral is called the Mohs hardness scale.

You can test a mineral's hardness by scratching it with different objects!

Diamonds are the hardest matter on Earth.

Pressure and more than 2,000°F (1,093°C) of heat turn carbon in the crust into diamonds. These minerals formed billions of years ago inside Earth's crust.

Raw diamonds look very different after they've been cut and shined, or polished. When a mineral is cut, polished, and used for decoration, it's called a gem.

FACT 11

The oldest emerald ever found is nearly 3 billion years old.

Emeralds are green or bluish-green gems made of a mineral called beryl. Like other gems, they usually form inside rocks. People have used emeralds as decoration for more than 4,000 years.

Getting a gem like an emerald out of the rock it formed in requires great skill!

Shake It Up

FACT 12

Most earthquakes happen less than 50 miles (80 km) below Earth's surface.

Deeper earthquakes also happen when one plate is pushed beneath another. This can happen as deep as 400 miles (640 km) below Earth's surface!

When Earth's plates push on each other, a lot of pressure builds up. When the plates suddenly move, the pressure is released and travels through Earth's crust in waves!

In May 1960, the largest earthquake ever recorded hit Chile!

Magnitude is a measure of the **energy** released in an earthquake. Chile's earthquake was a magnitude 9.5 out of 10! Earthquakes that strong destroy cities—and kill!

Earthquakes can be extremely dangerous—and deadly. Everything may look completely different after an earthquake hits!

Ring of Fire

As lava cools and hardens into rock, it changes and shapes the surrounding land—and even forms new land!

FACT 14

Almost all Earth's volcanoes are found along an area called the Ring of Fire.

The Ring of Fire is a special area that surrounds the Pacific Ocean. The edges of many of Earth's plates slide, crash, and pull away from each other here, causing volcanoes.

There are about 1,900 active volcanoes on Earth.

Active volcanoes are those that are likely to erupt—or explode with lava—again! Dormant volcanoes haven't erupted in a while, but could in the future. Extinct volcanoes will never erupt again.

The largest active volcano is Mauna Loa in Hawaii. The last time it erupted was in 1984. Could another eruption happen soon?

FACT 16

One-tenth of Earth is covered in ice!

This ice is in the form of glaciers, ice caps, and ice sheets.

Glaciers are huge masses of ice that move forward if more snow

and ice is added to them than what melts. They move back if

more snow and ice is lost than

what's added.

As Earth's **climate** gets warmer, scientists worry that the glaciers are melting too quickly. This could cause sea levels to rise so much that coastal cities end up underwater!

These mountains were created by glaciers!

As glaciers advance and retreat, they shape the land beneath them.

Once scientists figured out what shapes glaciers left behind as they moved across the land, they could map where glaciers traveled millions of years ago!

FACT 18

Rocks called fossils contain remains of animals and plants that lived millions of years ago.

Fossils form as layers of **sediment** pile on top of once-living plants and animals. Fossils teach us a great deal about life long ago!

As layers of sand, dirt, and other sediments pile up, they put pressure on the layers below and turn them into sedimentary rock.

Types of Fossils

mold fossil
a mark on the surface left in sediment that has become mineral over time

fossil in amber
a creature's whole body that's been trapped in sticky matter, such as sap. Sap that's hardened over thousands of years is called amber.

petrified wood
a piece of wood that had its matter replaced by minerals over thousands of years

trace fossil
something that shows how creatures lived, such as a track or poop

These are just some examples of the kinds of fossils that can be found all over the world!

In 2011, men digging in Canada found a dinosaur fossil with skin!

The 110-million-year-old fossil included scales, plates, and spikes. When it died, the nodosaur's body may have been pulled by a river into an ancient ocean and quickly buried under sediment.

Some say this nodosaur fossil is the best fossil of its kind ever found!

Fossils show that some animals that lived millions of years ago look pretty much the same today!

Horseshoe crabs, crocodiles, jellyfish, nautiluses, and sea sponges are examples of "living fossils." They haven't changed much at all for millions of years!

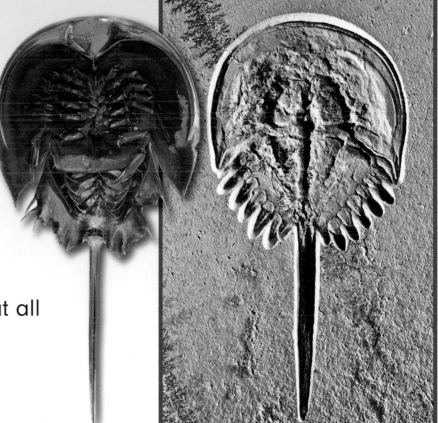

horseshoe crabs

You can see how this "living fossil" hasn't changed much in the millions of years it's lived on Earth.

Now that we have so many amazing tools, geology discoveries happen often. Sometimes these discoveries even make scientists rethink theories that have held true for hundreds of years! Right now, scientists are studying newly found sponge fossils that may tell us where all animals—including people—came from. Thanks to geology, our understanding of the world gets better every year.

From creatures that roamed Earth millions of years ago to glaciers melting today, geology is everywhere—and it rocks!

This sandstone shows layers and layers of Earth's past.

billion: one thousand million

climate: the average weather conditions of a place over a period of time

continent: one of the great divisions of land of Earth, such as North America, South America, Europe, Asia, Africa, Australia, or Antarctica

earthquake: a shaking of the ground caused by the movement of Earth's crust

energy: the power to do work

lava: melted rock from a volcano

pressure: a force that pushes on something else

sediment: material such as stone and sand that's carried into water by water or wind

temperature: how hot or cold something is

theory: an explanation based on facts that is generally accepted by scientists

volcano: an opening in Earth's crust through which lava flows

Books

Behrens, Janice. *Totally Cool Caves and Hot Volcanoes: +10 More Epic Landforms!* New York, NY: Children's Press, 2017.

Gray, Susan H. *Geology: The Study of Rocks.* New York, NY: Children's Press, 2012.

Woyt, Barbara A. *Geology.* New York, NY: Britannica Educational Publishing, 2017.

Websites

Geology 101
kids.nationalgeographic.com/explore/science/geology-101/#geology-sedimentary.jpg
Learn all about geology with this fun National Geographic article, written just for kids.

One Geology Kids
onegeology.org/extra/kids/what_is.html
Enjoy this website that brings important geology information together.

The Study of Our Earth
kidsgeo.com/geology-for-kids/
This in-depth online resource will teach you all about geology.

Index